The Great Divide

by Suzanne Slade

illustrated by Erin E. Hunter

Like people, most animals spend a lot of time with their family and friends. Many groups of animals have their own cool names. Have fun discovering animal group names while practicing your division skills too!

foxes – skulk

flamingos – stand

peacocks – muster

fish – school

penguins – rooker

squirrels – dray

llama – herd

lions – pride

wolves – pack

meerkats – mob

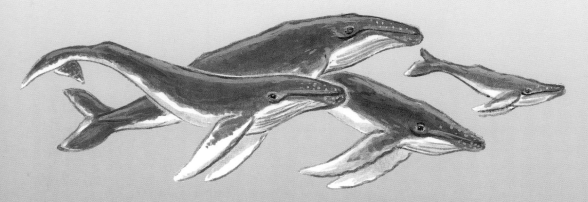

whales – pod

Ten baby leatherbacks
leave a sandy trail.
Five groups head for sea.
How many in each bale?

12 ÷ 4 =

welve tiny hummingbirds,
uzzing on a farm,
over near four flowers.
ow many in each charm?

÷ 3 = ?

ne hungry leopards
aking up from sleep.
hree groups are on the prowl.
ow many in each leap?

Twelve noisy mallard ducks
swimming down a stream
paddle into two long lines.
How many in each team?

12 ÷ 2 = ?

Six rambunctious rhinos
making quite a splash—
three mommas with their babies.
How many in each crash?

6 ÷ 3 = ?

$16 \div 2 = ?$

Sixteen busy wallabies—
moms always on the job.
Two groups hop away
how many in each mob?

Twenty tough gorillas,
magnificent and grand,
march in five directions.
How many in each band?

20 ÷ 5 = ?

$16 \div 4 = ?$

Sixteen shiny river toads,
in a sunny spot,
gather 'round four puddles.
How many in each knot?

15 ÷ 3 = ?

Fifteen playful elephants,
looking quite absurd,
perform in three rings.
How many in each herd?

Twenty stubborn billy goats,
lured by tasty bribes,
run into four pens.
How many in each tribe?

Fourteen hungry pelicans,
waiting by the dock,
find two tasty fish.
How many in each flock?

14 ÷ 2 = ?

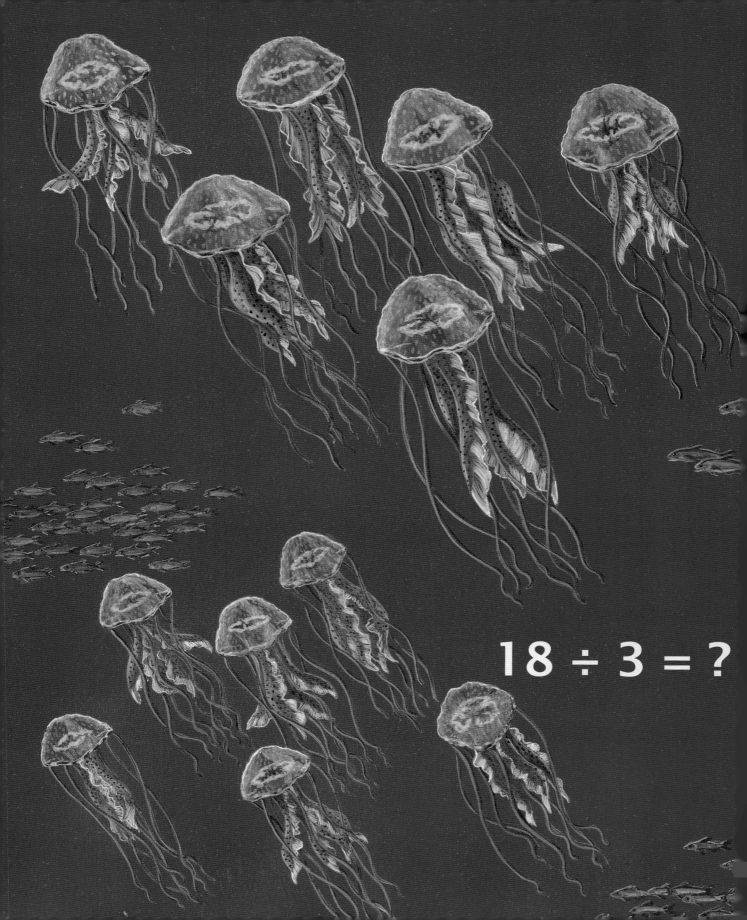

$18 \div 3 = ?$

**Eighteen purple jellyfish
dine on fishy snacks.
Three groups drift apart.
How many in each smack?**

For Creative Minds

Collective Nouns Matching

Match the animal with its collective noun (group name). Some group names are used mo than once.

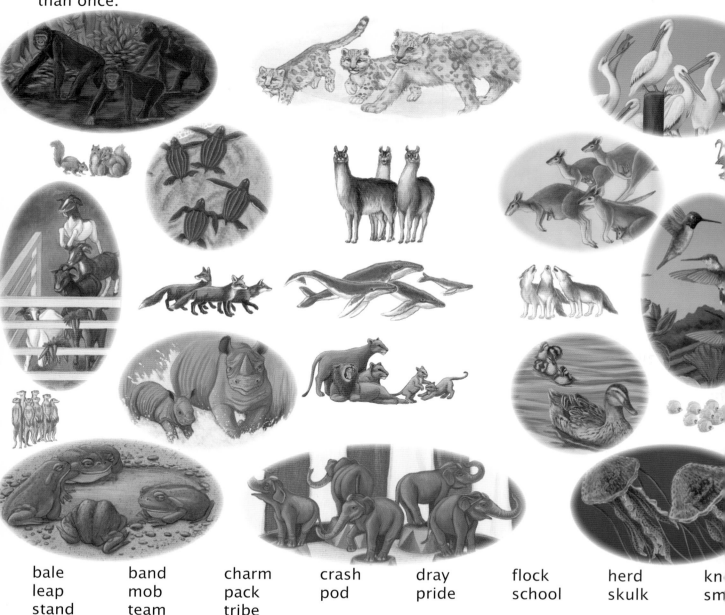

bale	band	charm	crash	dray	flock	herd	kn
leap	mob	pack	pod	pride	school	skulk	sm
stand	team	tribe					

ctive Nouns: gorillas-band; leopards-leap; pelicans-flock; squirrel-dray; seaturtles-bale; llamas-herd; wallabies-mob; ngos-stand; Billy goats-tribe; foxes-skulk; whales-pod; wolves-pack; hummingbirds-charm; meerkats-mob; rhinos- ; lions-pride; ducks-team; fish-school; toads-knot; elephants-herd; purple jellyfish-smack

Where in the World?

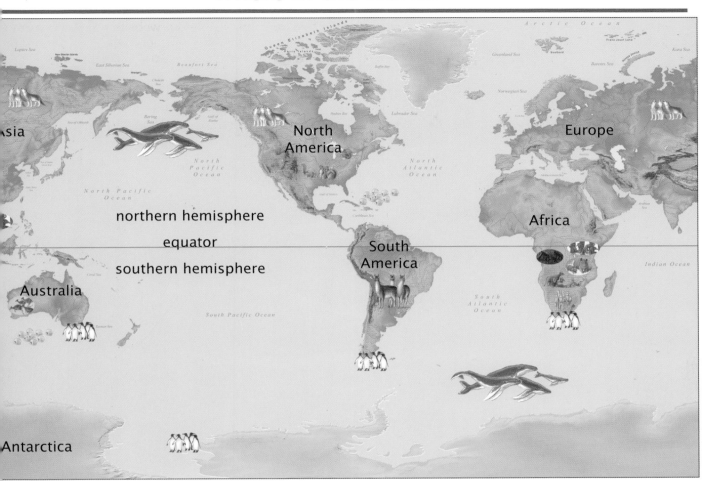

...nals live all over the world in all kinds of habitats. Some animals live on many continents ...e others live only on one or two continents. Some animals don't live on land at all—they ...ht live in freshwater lakes, rivers, or salty oceans.

Do whales live in rivers or in the ocean?

Meerkats, gorillas, and lions all live on which continent?

Name two continents where elephants live.

On what continent do wallabies live?

Which continent do llamas call home?

Are penguins found in the northern or southern hemisphere?

In which hemisphere do wolves live?

Which animals in this book live near you?

1. ocean; 2. Africa; 3. Africa and Asia; 4. Australia; 5. South America; 6. southern; 7. northern; 8. answers will vary

Hands On: Dividing Cookies

Division tells us how many equal groups there are or how many are in each group.

Suppose you have a dozen (12) cookies to share. How many cookies would each person get if there are 6 people, 4 people, 3 people or 2 people?

When dividing things into groups, the groups should be equal in number.

Suppose two people want to share the 12 cookies but one person takes 10 and gives 2 to the other person. Do you think the cookies were divided equally? Why or why not?

Division can also tell us into how many equal pieces something can be broken (fractions).

Break a cookie in half to give some to a friend. You just **divided** the cookie into two pieces!

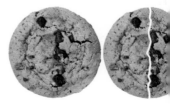

When using small numbers, it's easy to count how many cookies each person should get or how many animals are in each animal group. What happens when the numbers are big or you might not want to count? That's when knowing how to divide numbers is helpful.

Division: Opposite of Multiplication

vision is the opposite of multiplication, just as subtraction is the opposite of addition. The numbers being multiplied are called factors and the answer to a multiplication problem is called the product. In division, the factors are called divisors and the roduct is called the dividend. It doesn't matter which divisor is used first, the answer will always be the other divisor.

2 sea turtles in each bale x 5 bales of turtles = 10 sea turtles.
5 bales of sea turtles x 2 turtles in each bale = 10 sea turtles.
10 sea turtles ÷ 2 turtles in each bale = 5 bales of sea turtles.
10 sea turtles ÷ 5 bales of sea turtles = 2 sea turtles in each bale.

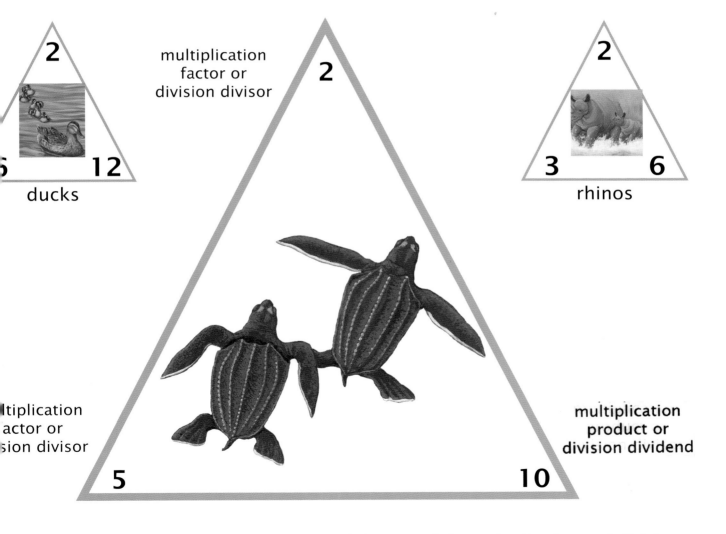

2

6   12

ducks

multiplication
factor or
division divisor

2

2

3   6

rhinos

ltiplication
actor or
sion divisor

multiplication
product or
division dividend

5   10

r printable cards to use as manipulatives and the rest of the multiplication and division ct family triangles, go to www.SylvanDellPublishing.com and click on the book's cover. From there, click on "teaching activities."

Library of Congress Cataloging-in-Publication Data

Slade, Suzanne.
  The great divide / by Suzanne Slade ; illustrated by Erin E. Hunter.
    p. cm. -- (What's new at the zoo?) (What's the difference?)
  ISBN 978-1-60718-521-5 (hardcover) -- ISBN 978-1-60718-530-7 (pbk.) -- ISBN 978-1-60718-539-0 (Englis
ebook) -- ISBN 978-1-60718-548-2 (Spanish ebook) 1. Division--Juvenile literature. 2. Animals--Infancy--
Juvenile literature. I. Hunter, Erin E., ill. II. Title.
  QA115.S639 2012
  513.2'14--dc23

                              2011032755

With love to Worth and Beverly Slade—SS

For my brothers, Colin and Andrew—EEH

Thanks to Hallsville ISD (TX) math teacher
Rachel Hilchey for reviewing the math-related
information in this book.

Manufactured in China, December, 2011
This product conforms to CPSIA 2008
First Printing
Published by Sylvan Dell Publishing
Mt. Pleasant, SC 29464

Also available as eBooks featuring auto-flip, auto-rea
3D-page-curling, and selectable English and Spanish
and audio

Interest level: 004-009 Grade level: P-4 640L

Curriculum keywords: collective nouns, equations/ma
symbols, maps, multiply/divide, rhythm or rhyme